SUSAN E. GOODMAN   MICHAEL J. DOOLITTLE

SKYSC

RAPER

FROM THE GROUND UP

ALFRED A. KNOPF   NEW YORK

To Elisa Petrini, who has always provided home
and hearth, help and heart, but especially during
this project. And to Mike, who seems at his
happiest up on the steel.
—S.E.G.

To Amity, Eliza, and Georgia, who put up with
many early mornings. Most of all to Harriette,
whose book this is.
—M.J.D.

THIS IS A BORZOI BOOK PUBLISHED BY ALFRED A. KNOPF

Text copyright © 2004 by Susan Goodman.

Photographs copyright © 2004 by Michael Doolittle.

All rights reserved under International and Pan-American Copyright Conventions. Published in the United
States of America by Alfred A. Knopf, an imprint of Random House Children's Books, a division of Random
House, Inc., New York, and simultaneously in Canada by Random House of Canada Limited, Toronto.
Distributed by Random House, Inc., New York. KNOPF, BORZOI BOOKS, and the colophon are registered
trademarks of Random House, Inc.

Library of Congress Cataloging-in-Publication Data
Goodman, Susan E., 1952–
Skyscraper : from the ground up / Susan Goodman ; photographs by Michael Doolittle.
p. cm.
ISBN 0-375-81309-8 (trade) — ISBN 0-375-91309-2 (lib. bdg.)
1. Skyscrapers—Juvenile literature. [1. Skyscrapers—Design and construction.]
I. Doolittle, Michael J., ill. II. Title.
TH1615.G66 2004   720'.483—dc22   2003027925

www.randomhouse.com/kids
MANUFACTURED IN CHINA
November 2004
10 9 8 7 6 5 4 3 2 1   First Edition

Look up.

A new tower of glass and steel is pushing into the sky.

Everyone is hard at work. Backhoe operators take giant bites out of the earth with their buckets. Ironworkers balance on steel beams like urban acrobats hundreds of feet above the ground. Sparks fly as welders use heat instead of hammers to attach giant pieces of steel.

Throughout the building, engineers, plumbers, and carpenters are doing their jobs. Together they will create something no one of them could make alone—a new skyscraper in New York City.

This building began, however, long before the first bulldozer rumbled onto the job.

"It starts off and you're just thinking about nuts and bolts and concrete and steel. Then at some point you stand back and see this thing soaring up into the air. The feeling . . . it's indescribable."
—Matt DiGiorgi, project manager

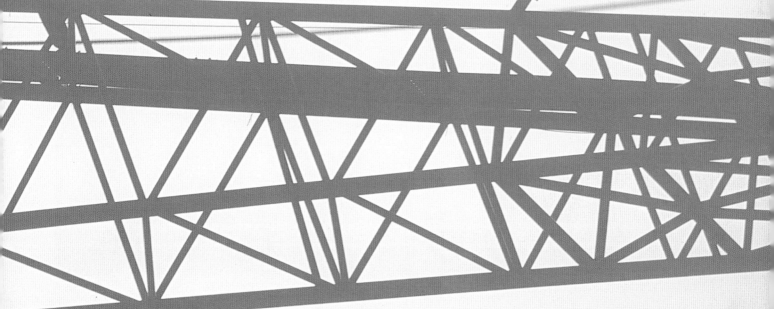

It takes thousands of people doing over 300 different jobs to make this building. . . . On busy days, 600 people can be working on the construction site. . . . Anyone who goes on-site must wear a hard hat. . . . The average hard hat weighs 14 ounces, just under a pound.

Some artists paint and draw. Architects are artists who sculpt the city.

Unlike other artists, architects can't make their projects look any way they want. They must design a building that is comfortable and safe. They must include ideas that owners have about their building. The city has its ideas too. City laws say a building's shape must fit in with its neighbors and allow the sun to reach the streets below.

The architect must juggle all these challenges. Plus one more. He wants the skyscraper to be beautiful.

Architect Gary Haney makes the skyscraper's outer walls the same height as the old buildings close by. The second, taller set of walls matches the height of its newer neighbors. This is his way of saying hello to the neighborhood before the tower in the middle proudly rises above the crowd.

Standing free, reflecting sun and clouds, this column of glass will become part of the sky.

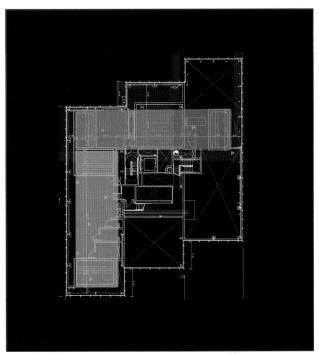

A team of architects, engineers, and experts on everything from parking to window washing helps Gary Haney design the skyscraper. . . . They create 60 different models before the building reaches its final design. . . . About 1,500 pages of construction plans are made to explain this design to the builders.

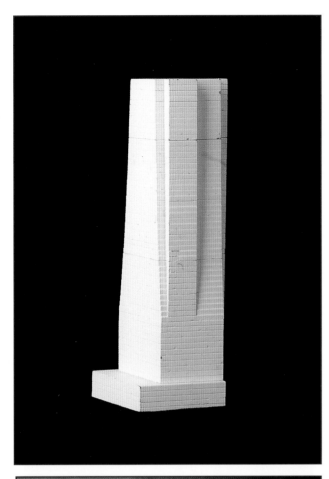

(left) This model shows all the possible building space permitted on the site by city law. Haney's job is to design the skyscraper that fits inside.

(above) The final design for the Random House building, home to a publishing company, looks like three books sandwiched between a pair of bookends.

(left) Haney begins thinking about a center section that shoots up from the street level.

Skyscrapers are so heavy that if they just sat on the ground, they would sink into the earth's crust. This skyscraper will stand upon bedrock beneath the earth's surface, rock so solid that it can support the 200 million pounds the building will weigh when full of furniture and people.

To get to bedrock and dig the basement, backhoes scoop out dirt and rock—up to seven tons in each bucket. Dump trucks, each carting off nearly fifty tons of the stuff, drive all the way to the neighboring state of New Jersey.

The hole grows, and workers prop up a neighboring hotel to keep it from falling in. In one corner, workers hit bedrock too soon; the basement needs to be deeper. They use the world's biggest hammer to punch through. Each blow is so hard that it makes waves in toilets a block away.

Even after the basement's hole is finished, there are places where workers must keep digging to reach bedrock. After they do, they fill these spots with steel and concrete to make them especially strong. Then they cover the holes with steel-and-concrete platforms.

"It seems so easy when you look at the drawings, but then you start digging. You never really know what's down there till you start."
—Mohammed Bouisetta, engineer

To empty the hole, trucks cart away 2,000 loads of dirt. . . . The 17,000-pound hammer hits with about a million pounds of force; seven of them would match the force of a space shuttle liftoff. . . . The hole for the basement is forty feet deep and almost a city block wide—so big that using a garden hose to fill it like a swimming pool would take over four and a half years.

"Problems, deadlines . . . you never think in terms of 'no' or 'can't.' If it has to be done, we figure out a way to do it."
—Billy Rogers, project superintendent

Early one Saturday morning, a monstrous crane parks on a busy city street. Police put up roadblocks and wave stubborn drivers away. New York will give up this street for just one weekend. Workers have only two days to build a smaller crane, which will be used inside the construction site.

First the giant crane lowers a dozen 20-ton columns to be bolted into place. Later these columns will be part of the frame that holds up the skyscraper. Now they will support the new crane.

The giant crane works day and night, stretching its long arm, or boom, into the site with pieces of the new crane. Workers build its seven-story tower, then its frame, then the red cab where its operator will sit. Finally, late Sunday evening, they attach the boom that will spend the next two years lifting the skyscraper's steel frame into position.

The giant crane has a lifting capacity of 500 tons. . . . Its boom can stretch 164 feet, more than half a football field. . . . The new crane can lift 50 tons.

Piece by piece, the steel frame climbs upward. Its columns stand tall and strong, connected by beams stretching in between. Every piece is individually designed to support the weight in its part of the building. And it wears a number that pinpoints where it fits into the frame.

Each ironworker in the raising crew does his part to put the steel where it belongs. The foreman decides which piece is next. The hooker-on lassoes it with a cable and . . .

Up it goes!

The signalman is the crane operator's second set of eyes as the beam crosses the sky. "Boom up, swing left," he calls until the beam is almost in place.

Two connectors stand at opposite sides of the beam and bring it home. They heave and hammer until the holes in the new beam and in the waiting columns are lined up well enough to jam a few bolts in place.

Working the steel is a risky business. Hard hats and harnesses help combat the danger. Still, says one ironworker, "standing on a beam fifty stories high lets you know you're alive."

"You'd think being the signalman is easy, but making sure a beam doesn't knock your guys into a thirty-story freefall . . . I'd say *that's* stressful."
—Mike Emerson, signalman

Ironworkers ride hoists, or work elevators, to get to the top of the frame. . . . The bottom columns, which support most of the building's weight, are so thick that they weigh 730 pounds per foot. . . . Higher up, some columns weigh 53 pounds per foot. . . . Connectors wear 50 pounds of equipment around their waist, which helps weigh them down. On windy days, they add bolts as extra weight to help them balance.

"If you're afraid of heights, this ain't for you. But people in this building are going to pay a lot of money for the view that I see every day."
—Sean McGloin, crane-operating engineer

Next, plumber-uppers use cables to pull the columns plumb, a straight up-and-down position. The bolter-uppers follow, adding the rest of the bolts—up to one hundred at a single connection. Then the welders lower their hoods and finish the job by fusing some of the joints together.

When work on one floor is finished, the ironworkers help jack the crane higher to start the next. Ironworkers are a building's pioneers. Nothing is up there but sky . . . until they bring in the steel.

It takes 258,000 bolts to fasten the steel together. . . . There are 9,000 separate pieces of steel in the frame. . . . All together, they weigh about 12,000 tons—as much as a herd of 4,000 elephants. . . . The heaviest piece is a girder on the 26th floor that weighs 82,000 pounds.

The skyscraper's core is a cluster of its strongest columns. The core runs from the basement to the rooftop and supports half of the building's weight. If the steel frame is a skyscraper's skeleton, the core is its backbone. It keeps the building standing straight.

The core also houses a building's elevators and stairways. Steel and elevators are two of three innovations from the late 1800s that made skyscrapers possible. Brick walls couldn't support the weight of buildings much taller than five stories. To climb higher than ten stories, stone walls would be so thick that they'd crowd the building's interior. But when a building has a steel frame, the sky's the limit. And elevators can shoot people up to the top, however high it is.

The other innovation? It was the electric lightbulb. Buildings could grow bigger once they had lights to brighten up rooms without windows.

A single core column must support over 10 million pounds of building. . . . About 2,500 people will ride these elevators every day. . . . The fastest of the 21 elevators in this building can travel 20 miles per hour. . . . If all the elevator shafts were lined up, they'd stretch over a mile and a quarter. . . . Each year, these elevators will travel over 30,000 miles, much farther than a trip around the world.

"It might be money that starts a project, but it's pride that builds and finishes it."
—Bob Henesy, site-safety manager

This skyscraper is like two buildings, one on top of the other. Its lower half will be business offices and has a steel frame. Starting on the 27th story, the skyscraper becomes an apartment building. This part uses a concrete frame, which is faster and easier to make.

Carpenters begin each of these stories by building a wooden platform to support the new concrete floor. Then they build wooden walls, molds for the concrete columns. They put steel frames inside to make the columns stronger. At street level, a powerful pump pushes heavy concrete hundreds of feet up through a hose. Masons pour it into the molds for the columns. They finish by pouring the floor—eight inches of concrete and steel bars.

The following day, the concrete is dry enough to remove the wood framing. Then it's time to start the next story.

"When you're pouring all day, concrete builds up on your pants and boots—maybe ten pounds' worth. You change to go home and you've got a new spring in your step."
—Andrew Lewis, mason

The spot where concrete mixers park to deliver their loads is made ten times stronger than the rest of the basement floor. . . . It takes about a week to erect one story of steel frame and three days for a concrete one. . . . There's enough concrete in this skyscraper to build over 84 miles of four-foot-wide sidewalks. . . . This is only the second building ever constructed in New York City to combine steel and concrete frames.

"Up here, on windy days, we try to pick stuff up so it doesn't go over the side. But you've got to be careful. A sheet of plywood can catch the wind and sail like a kite. If you don't let go, you go with it."
—Kevin Scally, ironworker

Building in New York is like getting dressed in a broom closet—not enough room and too much stuff in the way. Temporary offices for the construction company sit above the sidewalk, and outdoor toilets are stuffed into corners. Workers build walls pressed up against neighboring buildings. Nets called "diapers" keep bolts and concrete from falling on pedestrians below. And deep in the subway, engineers use a seismograph, the same machine that measures earthquakes, to make sure pounding doesn't damage the tunnel.

With no room to store materials, deliveries must be timed perfectly. The day's steel arrives each morning, trucked in at night so it doesn't block traffic. Concrete mixers are ordered precisely when needed. Once loaded, they only have 90 minutes to travel through town and traffic before their contents harden.

If a work elevator isn't put in the right place, all the extra seconds of carrying materials where they're needed can add $500,000 to the cost of the job. . . . At the height of construction, the site has seven portable toilets that are emptied twice a week.

As the frame climbs upward, workers begin hanging the curtain wall below. Only two clips attach each panel to the beams. Then gravity presses the panel into its frame and keeps it in place.

Unlike a house's outer walls, a curtain wall doesn't hold up any weight. If the steel frame is a skyscraper's skeleton, the curtain wall is its skin. Like our skin, it protects what's inside from wind and rain and cold.

A curtain wall also becomes the face a skyscraper presents to the world. Its materials help create the building's personality. The stone on the Random House building is serious. It creates strong, reliable bookends for the exciting glass "books" inside.

"There's a point when hundreds of workers are creating your vision; something that was in your mind is taking shape right on the street. It's cool, but also a little scary."
—Gary Haney, architect

The curtain-wall panels weigh from 1,300 to 3,000 pounds apiece. . . .The finished curtain wall contains 2,186 windows. . . . Its stone is only one inch thick. . . . If you made a ten-foot-wide column out of the curtain wall, it would stretch seven miles into the sky.

"I've learned that no matter how bad a crisis, the sun will still come up tomorrow. But I used to go crazy. Once I woke from a dream, yanking on my wife's wrist and yelling, 'This is the wrong handrail!' My wife just looked at me and said, 'Time for an attitude adjustment.'"
—Billy Rogers, project superintendent

Strong winds make a skyscraper sway like a tree. A few feet of movement is fine, but more would make the people inside feel seasick. The building's core helps it stay sturdy. And up on its 50th floor, two 90-foot tanks stretch across the building—one east to west, the other north to south. The water in these tanks totals one and a half million pounds. When the building starts moving to the west, for example, this very heavy water doesn't want to move with it. The water pushes on the eastern side of the skyscraper, which slows the building down.

To protect the building against fire, a mason covers the steel with fireproofing so it can't get too hot and bend. On the top floor, a water tower is also ready to fill the skyscraper's fire hoses. When the pipefitters test the system's water pressure, pedestrians a block away open their umbrellas.

If the city loses electricity, the skyscraper's emergency generator can make enough to run elevators, emergency lights, and fire pumps. When working, this generator vibrates so much that if it didn't rest on shock absorbers, it would crumple its corner of the building.

Ladders on fire trucks can't reach higher than eight stories, which is one reason why skyscrapers need their own defense. . . . The water tower holds 17,000 gallons, enough water to fill 340 bathtubs. . . . The emergency generator weighs 38,000 pounds, as much as 13 Volkswagen Beetles.

The electrical and mechanical systems use up 30 percent of the skyscraper's construction budget. . . . If fused together, the pipes for the skyscraper's sprinkler system alone would stretch 170 miles. . . . A carpenter can Sheetrock an office in less than 30 minutes. . . . Tilers install 171,000 tiles in bathrooms and kitchens throughout the building. . . . Carpenters use 600,000 pieces of wood for the floors. . . . Plumbers install over 400 toilets throughout the building.

A secret world of pipes and cables runs through the skyscraper. These systems run from the roof to the basement and above the ceiling of each story.

If a steel frame is a skyscraper's skeleton, the mechanical and electrical systems are its lungs and guts and nervous system. Fans and ducts bring fresh air into the building and take stale air out. Some pipes bring clean water to sinks and water fountains, others carry waste to the sewer. Cables bring light and the Internet to every corner of the building.

Getting these systems in place is a huge job. Just threading the electrical cable through pipes called conduits takes a year and a half. And if you tied all the electrical wiring in this building together, it would stretch from New York City to California.

Once these systems are installed, other workers start dividing floors into rooms, putting up Sheetrock for walls and ceilings, smoothing it over with plaster, and painting it. They use frosted glass to give privacy to offices, lay carpets, and put tiles, sinks, and toilets into bathrooms. Floor by floor, they turn a steel-and-concrete shell into a place where people can work and live.

"This skyscraper is like a huge, closed box. If this box was only thirty-five degrees inside or dark or without fresh air, people couldn't work here. My job is to make it comfortable."
—Manny Moayer, mechanical engineer

Three and a half years after the first bulldozer rolled onto the lot, the skyscraper is finally finished. Now incoming trucks deliver new furniture and food for the cafeteria—not concrete or steel. Office workers hunch over their computers. People in the apartments take showers and cook dinner. Customers open accounts at a bank on the ground floor.

Our skyscraper has become a part of New York— the city that has been nicknamed "Skyscraper National Park."

In 1888, the 11-story Tower Building was New York's first metal frame skyscraper. Since then, New York has been building in five directions—north, south, east, west, and *up*. Today, almost 5,000 skyscrapers proudly crowd into the city skyline.

"My grandfather worked on the Empire State Building, and my dad built the Verrazano Narrows Bridge. I worked on the World Trade Center. Sometimes I look around and think, 'Yup, we helped make this city.'"
—Mike Emerson, signalman

New York has more skyscrapers over 270 feet tall than any other city. . . . Our skyscraper is 678 feet tall, with 52 stories aboveground and two below, including a parking garage with car elevators. . . . It has 860,044 square feet of floor area—two banks, 25 stories of offices, and 130 apartments.

The high cost of land in New York has pushed its buildings into the sky. But we build up there for a second reason—because we can. As the famous architect Philip Johnson once said, "I'm not just creating forms. I'm creating attitudes."

Skyscrapers are tall. The fact that we can build them makes us feel tall—tall enough to touch the sky.

The Empire State Building, at 102 stories and 1,453 feet, was the tallest building in the world for over 40 years. . . . Now the tallest building in the world, Taipei 101 in Taiwan, is 101 stories, 1,667 feet high . . . . Experts say skyscrapers can still climb much, much higher.

AROUND THE WORLD

This skyscraper is in New York City, but the materials to build it came from all over the world. The stone for the curtain wall, for example, was carved from a quarry in Canada, then sent to Spain to be cut and polished. Shipped to Tennessee, it was made into panels with glass begun in Texas and finished in Mexico and metal mined in Australia and processed in China.

The world in one building . . .

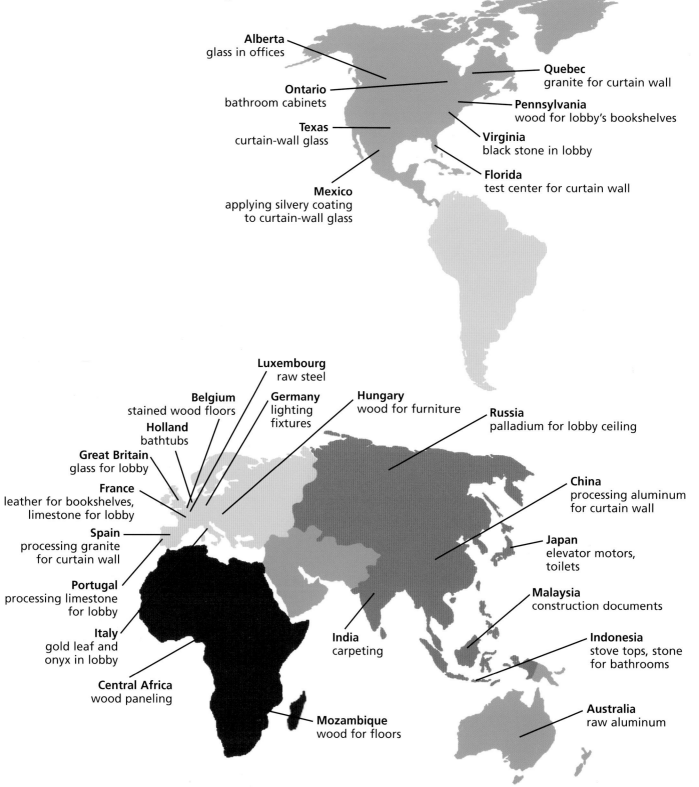

Alberta
glass in offices

Quebec
granite for curtain wall

Ontario
bathroom cabinets

Pennsylvania
wood for lobby's bookshelves

Texas
curtain-wall glass

Virginia
black stone in lobby

Mexico
applying silvery coating
to curtain-wall glass

Florida
test center for curtain wall

Luxembourg
raw steel

Belgium
stained wood floors

Germany
lighting
fixtures

Hungary
wood for furniture

Russia
palladium for lobby ceiling

Holland
bathtubs

Great Britain
glass for lobby

China
processing aluminum
for curtain wall

France
leather for bookshelves,
limestone for lobby

Spain
processing granite
for curtain wall

Japan
elevator motors,
toilets

Portugal
processing limestone
for lobby

Malaysia
construction documents

Italy
gold leaf and
onyx in lobby

India
carpeting

Indonesia
stove tops, stone
for bathrooms

Central Africa
wood paneling

Mozambique
wood for floors

Australia
raw aluminum

GLOSSARY

Beam—a horizontal piece of the steel frame

Bedrock—solid rock that is part of the earth's crust

Boom—the arm of a crane, which helps move heavy objects

Column—a vertical piece of the steel frame

Conduit—a plastic or metal pipe that holds cables

Core—the strongest part of the skyscraper's skeleton

Curtain wall—panels that hang on the building's skeleton and form its outer wall

Elevator shaft—an opening running through the floors of a building, which provides the path for an elevator

Foundation—the base that supports the building

Framework—the steel skeleton of the building

Girder—a main beam that helps support vertical weight

Hoist—a work elevator used to lift heavy loads

Interior—the inside of the building

Mason—a worker who builds with stone, brick, or cement

ACKNOWLEDGMENTS

It takes an army of people to build a skyscraper and certainly a battalion or two to help write a book about one. From architects and engineers to plumbers and ironworkers—we thank all the people in offices and on-site who answered our endless questions.

We would especially like to thank Gary Haney and Chris Fogarty at Skidmore, Owings & Merrill; Plaza Construction's Michael Fitzmaurice, Billy Rogers, Steve Bunzel, Lee Houck, Marco Sulihan, Richard Wood, and Matt DiGiorgi, to whom we are grateful for his careful review of the manuscript; Andrew Pattap and Richard Loccicero at the Related Companies; Mohammed Bouisetta and Akbar Tamboli at Thornton-Tomasetti Engineers; "Safety Bob" Henesy; Joe Martinelli at Northside Concrete; Jeffrey Gannett at ADF Steel Corp.; Steve Kinnaman at Jaros Baum & Bolles; Bhaskar Srivastava at Ismael Leyva Architects; Fred Bauerschmidt at Bauerschmidt & Sons; Manny Moayer and Peter Costa at Cosentini Associates; and Patrick Dumphey and all the other electrical and plumbing contractors, who helped total up the miles of materials in this building.

At Random House, Harriette Dorsen was right there from the beginning, Kim Bertin pitched in along the way, and then Michelle Frey, Michele Burke, and Sarah Hokanson stepped in and helped us finish this book so beautifully.

Out of New York City, thanks to Deborah Hirschland and Robie Harris for being such wise readers. And to Don Heiny, who helped whittle down 10,000 photographs.

The photographs on page 11 of the computer rendering and model view are courtesy of Skidmore, Owings & Merrill LLP.